Heinemann Educational Books Ltd
22 Bedford Square, London WC1B 3HH

LONDON  EDINBURGH  MELBOURNE  AUCKLAND
HONG KONG  SINGAPORE  KUALA LUMPUR  NEW DELHI
NAIROBI  JOHANNESBURG  IBADAN  KINGSTON
EXETER (NH)  PORT OF SPAIN

ISBN  0 435 23600 8

Typeset by The Castlefield Press of Northampton,
and printed and bound in Great Britain by
Spottiswoode Ballantyne of Colchester and London

# CONTENTS

# INTRODUCTION

*by Keith Miles*

The English mystery plays are themselves shrouded in mystery. Their precise origins are unknown, their authors are largely unidentified, and the details of their presentation are still a matter for conjecture. What is certain is this: the plays must not be dismissed as the poor relations of our dramatic history. They are among the crowning achievements of late medieval literature.

The first mention of the Coventry Mystery Plays is in 1392 when the Drapers' Company, which performed *Doomsday*, is known to have used a tenement in Little Park Street as a pageant house. It is probable that some of the plays, if not the full cycle, were in existence before this date because mystery plays were a well-established phenomenon in the fourteenth century. One recalls the merry clerk, Absolon, in *The Miller's Tale*, trying everything to impress his beloved Alison:

Sometyme, to shew his lightnesse and maistyre
He playeth Herodes on a scaffold hye;

And there is ample evidence from other sources of the popularity of the mystery plays in the major towns and cities of Chaucer's England.

Medieval drama was born within the confines of the Church. Dramatic episodes from the Bible had been incorporated into the liturgy for hundreds of years. They were in Latin and were performed by members of the clergy in a holy place. Mystery plays, by contrast, were in the vernacular and presented by lay actors in public places. This made possible the use of material — the demonic ranting of Herod, for example, or the coarse banter of the Torturers — that would have been outright blasphemy inside a church.

Mystery plays were performed for the most part on the Feast of Corpus Christi, which fell on the Thursday after Trinity Sunday and which marked the completion of the sacrifice to Christ. Since the Feast occurred in June, the trades guilds who presented the plays could count on a long day and — Deo volente — fine weather. These were important factors in view of the scale of the cycles of plays. The Chester cycle, comprising twenty-four plays, took three days to perform and the citizens of York, eager to make use of every minute of light, used to begin their first play at 4.30 a.m. Coventry was something of an exception in that its shorter cycle — ten pageants in all — could be staged in one day.

The Coventry Mystery Plays were the most famous in England and this is reflected in the number of royal visitors they attracted. Henry V, Henry VI, Richard III and Henry VIII are all known to have attended the annual performances. In 1457 Queen Margaret is said to have been peeved when she was unable to see the full cycle of plays. Darkness prevented the performance of *Doomsday* and she had to be content with only nine of the pageants.

Evidence suggests that fewer crafts supported the plays in Coventry than elsewhere. Again, some of the guilds combined to produce a particular pageant. An act of Coventry leet passed in 1445 gives us some indication of the way certain guilds combined, and also shows the order of procession through the city on the morning of Corpus Christi Day:

> Pur le ridyng on Corpus xpi day and for watch on midsomer even: The furst craft, fysshers and cokes; baxters and milners; bochers; whittawers and glovers; pynners, tylers and wrights; skynners; barkers; corvysers; smythes; wevers; wirdrawers; cardemakers, sadelers, peyntours and masons; gurdelers; taylors, walkers and sheremen; deysters; drapers; mercers.

Of the ten pageants that made up the Coventry cycle, only two survive — *The Pageant of the Shearmen and Taylors* and *The Weavers' Pageant.* I have worked from the texts as reprinted in 1825 by Thomas Sharp, the antiquarian, in his *Dissertation on the Pageants or Dramatic Mysteries, Anciently performed at Coventry, by the Trading Companies of that City*. Sharp himself worked directly from copies made in 1534 by one Robert Croo, who had been involved with the promotion of the plays for a number of years. The manuscript of *The Pageant of the Shearmen and Taylors* was destroyed in a fire at the Birmingham Free Library in 1879, but Croo's original draft of *The Weavers' Pageant* has survived and is kept in the Coventry City Record Office. It is a fascinating document, written on parchment in secretary hand and dating from the eve of a Reformation that was to alter the whole official view of the presentation of mystery plays.

In preparing this version of the two pageants, I have tried to make them accessible to a modern audience without sacrificing the spirit of the original. It should be stressed that this is an acting version and that certain changes have been made for theatrical reasons. The Prologue, spoken by Joseph in performance, was specially written to draw the audience in to the first acting area. In *The Pageant of the Shearmen and Taylors* there is a short Prophet Play or Learned Dialogue which links the visit of the Three Shepherds with the first Herod scene. We found it more effective to assign this section — Scene Four here — to the First Shepherd and a crowd which included a prophet. Similarly, the Prophet Play which introduces *The Weavers' Pageant* was found to have more impact when shortened and spoken by the two soldiers left onstage after Herod's hasty departure into Egypt — Scene Eleven here.

Unlike most of the plays in the other cycles, the Coventry pageants deal with more than one subject. *The Pageant of the Shearmen and Taylors* takes the story from the Annunciation to the Massacre of the Innocents in a series of fast-moving and vivid scenes. Notable features of this pageant are the characterisation of Joseph as a tetchy and comic old man who reacts badly to the news of impending parenthood; the ranting flamboyance of Herod, 'cheff capten of hell'; and the roles both of the mothers (who sing the Coventry Carol) and of the soldiers during the

Massacre. There is a fine irony in the fact that Herod is first introduced by a Herald who speaks in medieval French — the language of chivalry. *The Weavers' Pageant* deals with the Purification and with the Disputation in the Temple. The comedy of Joseph's situation is more fully exploited in this pageant and his complaints are set against the practical and determined character of Mary. There is evidence to suggest that the episode where the twelve-year-old Jesus confounds the Doctors in the Temple was the most popular of all the plays with Coventry audiences, not least because of its use of dramatic irony.

Since the Coventry Mysteries end with Jesus as a boy of twelve, I have added scenes from the other cycles to continue the story through to the Resurrection, thus giving a more complete theatrical and religious experience. I have tried to select those extracts most in keeping with the style of the Coventry pageants, and in some cases — the Baptism, the Betrayal and the Trial — sections from more than one cycle have been joined together. For the Betrayal, some dialogue was lifted bodily from the Gospel of St Mark.

The other cycles represented here are the York cycle; the Chester cycle; the Towneley cycle, which hails from Wakefield in Yorkshire but which takes its name from the Lancashire family who kept the manuscripts of the plays for a number of years; and the Ludus Coventriae, wrongly attributed to Coventry and more likely to have come from the East Midlands. All these cycles contain material from the Old Testament and trace the story from the Creation to the Last Judgement. The Coventry pageants were thought to be distinctive in that they contained only New Testament material, but this view has now been revised by some scholars. As Professor Hardin Craig has urged, '. . . such renowned subjects as the Creation, Cain and Abel, Noah and the Flood, and probably Abraham and Isaac must have been performed at Coventry because of their popularity elsewhere, and because the idea of a Corpus Christi play demands a fall of man as well as a redemption.' (Supplement to the Introduction to *Two Coventry Corpus Christi Plays*, 1957 edition.)

This version was first produced in the ruins of the old Coventry

Cathedral on 1 August 1978. It was presented by the Belgrade Theatre in association with Coventry Cathedral and received generous sponsorship from a number of firms in the city. The exciting and imaginative production, which used the whole cathedral as an acting area, was by Ed Thomason, to whom this publication is dedicated.

# LIST OF CHARACTERS

A Prologue

The Prophet Isaiah

The Virgin Mary

The Angel Gabriel

Joseph

Three Shepherds

A Prophet

Three Women

A Herald

Herod

Three Kings

Three Soldiers

Simeon

Anna

A Clerk

Three Doctors

Jesus

John the Baptist

A Blind Boy — Chelidonius

Crowd

His Sister

John ⎫

Peter ⎬ Jesus' Disciples

Judas ⎭

Two Neighbours

Two Pharisees

Two Jews

Mary of Bethany

Martha

Lazarus

Three Burghers

A Lame Man

A Messenger

Caiaphas

Annas

Pilate

Four Torturers

A Centurion

# The Coventry Mystery Plays

## *PROLOGUE*

Lordings, royal and reverent,
Lovely ladies now here present,
Worthy citizens, it is our intent
To play the Life of Christ here.
The worshipful actors of this town,
Small in number, great in renown,
Blessed by church and by mayoral gown,
Beseech you — all draw near!

## THE PAGEANT OF THE SHEARMEN AND TAYLORS

ISAIAH:

The Sovereign that sees every secret,
May he save you all and make you perfect and
  strong,
And give you grace with His mercy to meet!
For now in great misery mankind is bound,
The Serpent having given us so mortal a wound
That no creature can obtain for us release
Till God's true unction shall Judah seize.
Then will much mirth and joy increase,
And the right root in Israel spring
That shall bring forth the grain of wholeness;
And out of danger He shall us bring
Into that region where He is king,
Who far above all others does abound.
And that cruel Satan he shall confound.

1

Therefore I come upon this ground
To comfort every creature of birth;
For I, Isaiah the Prophet, have found
Many sweet matters wherein we may make mirth
In this same wise;
For although Adam be deemed to death,
With all his children, as Abel and Seth,
Yet ECCE VIRGO CONCIPIET —
Look where a remedy will rise!

Behold a maid shall conceive a child,
And get us more grace than ever man had,
Yet her maidenhead will not be defiled.
She is chosen to bear the Son of Almighty God.
His glorious birth shall redeem man again
From bondage and thrall.
Now be merry every man,
For the Lord is coming, who shall save us all!

*Exit*

## SCENE I: NAZARETH

THE VIRGIN MARY *is alone.* THE ANGEL
GABRIEL *appears before her and she is amazed*

GABRIEL:
Hail, Mary, full of grace!
The Lord God be with thee;
Above all women that ever was,
Lady, blessed may you be!

MARY:
Almighty father and king of bliss,
From all distresses save me now!

GABRIEL:
Dread thee nothing, maiden, of this;
From Heaven above have I been sent
On embassy from that king of bliss,

2

Unto thee, lady and virgin reverent,
Saluting thee here as most excellent,
Whose virtue above all others does abound.
Thou shalt conceive upon this ground
The Second Person in Trinity.
He will be born of thee alone.
Thy grace and goodness will never be gone,
But ever to live in virginity.

MARY:

I marvel greatly how that may be.
I never knew yet man's company.

GABRIEL:

The Holy Ghost on thee shall light,
And shadow thy soul soon with virtue
From the Father that is on height;
These words, fair maid, they are all true.

MARY:

Now that it be the Lord's will
His high pleasure to fulfil,
As his handmaid, I submit me.

(*Exit* ANGEL GABRIEL. JOSEPH, *an old man, enters*)

JOSEPH:

Mary, my wife so dear,
How are you, dame, and what cheer
Is with you this tide?

MARY:

Truly, husband, I am here,
Our Lord's will to abide.

(JOSEPH *looks at her more closely and is alarmed*)

JOSEPH:

What! Tell me, woman, what have you done?
Who has been with you while I was gone?

3

MARY:

> Neither man nor man's equal has been here,
> But only the Lord God's messenger.

JOSEPH:

> Say not so, woman! For shame, I cry!
> You are with child — against all right.
> Alas, that ever with his eye
> Joseph should see this sight!
> Tell me, woman, whose is the child?

MARY:

> None but yours, my husband mild,
> And that will be seen, certainly.

JOSEPH:

> But mine? Mine? Why say you so?
> Alas, alas! Mary, now must I go,
> Beguiled as many another may be.

MARY:

> No, truly, sir, you are not beguiled,
> There is no stain of sin, I am not defiled.
> Trust it well, husband.

JOSEPH:

> Husband, in faith! He is sad and cold.
> Poor Joseph, as you are old,
> Like a trusting fool now may you stand.
> All old men take example from me.
> How I am beguiled here, you may see,
> To wed so young a child.

(*He walks away*)

> Now farewell, Mary, I leave you here alone.
> Woe betide you, dame, for what you have done!

(MARY *sits down sadly.* JOSEPH *makes a short journey but tires and stops*)

4

This deed has filled me with so much grief,
That my steps grow weary, I am out of breath.
No further may I go.

(JOSEPH *lies down to sleep.* ANGEL GABRIEL
*appears*)

GABRIEL:
Arise up, Joseph, and go home again
Unto Mary, thy wife, so true to thee.
Comfort her now and think not of shame,
For, Joseph, a maiden still is she,
And has conceived without treachery
The Second Person in the Trinity.
Jesus shall His name be called,
And He shall save all this world.
Be not aghast.

JOSEPH:
Now, Lord, I thank you with heart full sad,
For of these things I am so glad
That all my care away is cast.
I will return to Mary in haste.

(GABRIEL *disappears.* JOSEPH *hurries back to*
MARY)

JOSEPH:
Ah, Mary, Mary, I kneel down low.
Forgive me, sweet wife, here in this land.
Mercy, Mary, for now I know
Of your good governance and how it doth stand.

MARY:
Now that Lord in Heaven, sir, may He forgive you!
And I do forgive you in His name
For evermore.

JOSEPH:
Truly, sweet wife, to you I say the same.

5

Now to Bethlehem must I be gone
To show myself. But full of care
Am I to leave you like this alone.
God knows, dame, how you should fare.

MARY:

Go boldly, husband, fear no thing,
For I will walk with you on the way.
I trust in God, Almighty King,
To speed us on our journey.

(*They gather up a few things and set off*)

JOSEPH:

I thank thee, Mary, for your goodness sweet.
My harsh words you do not blame.
Towards Bethlehem we shall set our feet,
Go we together in God's holy name.

(*They continue their journey*)

## SCENE 2:  ROAD NEAR BETHLEHEM

MARY *and* JOSEPH *pause to rest from travel*

JOSEPH:

Now to Bethlehem have we leagues three,
The day is nearly spent, it draws towards night;
At your ease, dame, I want you to be,
For you grow all weary, if I judge aright.

MARY:

Unto some place, Joseph, kindly lead,
So that I might rest with grace at this tide.

JOSEPH:

Blessed Mary, here will you stay.
For help to town will I now go.
What say you, dame? Is this not the best way?

MARY:

God have mercy, Joseph, my husband so meek!
And earnestly, I pray you, go now from me.

JOSEPH:

That shall be done in haste, Mary so sweet.
I will get some help as soon as may be.

(JOSEPH *goes out quickly.* MARY *goes off in the
opposite direction to await his return.* THE FIRST
SHEPHERD *enters, searching for his sheep*)

SHEPHERD I:

Now God who is in Trinity
May You save my fellows and me!
For I know not where my sheep be
This night. It is so cold.
What ho, fellows! Hoo! Hooe! Hoo!

(*Two more* SHEPHERDS *enter and listen*)

SHEPHERD II:

Hark, Sim. I hear our brother on the hill.

SHEPHERD III:

Let us follow his call if we will.

(*They call to the* FIRST SHEPHERD *as they head
towards him. He welcomes them with an embrace*)

SHEPHERD I:

Ah friends, a gust of wind brought a sudden mist,
And I was so completely lost
That I was sore afraid.

(*The* THIRD SHEPHERD *sees the star*)

SHEPHERD III:

Brothers, look up and behold!
What thing is yonder that shines so bright?

SHEPHERD II:
>Loved be God, most of might,
>That we have the grace to see this sight!

SHEPHERD I:
>Now gentle brothers, go we hence
>To worship that child of high magnificence,
>And that we may sing in His presence
>ET IN TERRA PAX OMNIBUS.

(*The* FIRST SHEPHERD *plays a note on his pipe,
then all three of them sing*)

SHEPHERDS:
>As I rode out this last night
>Of three jolly shepherds I saw a sight,
>And all about their fold a star shone bright;
>They sang terli terlow;
>So merrily the shepherds their pipes can blow.

>Down from Heaven, from Heaven so high,
>Of angels there came a great company;
>With mirth and joy and great solemnity.
>They sang terli terlow.
>So merrily the shepherds their pipes can blow.

(*They hear the sound of Angels singing 'Gloria in
excelsis Deo' and look up amazed*)


## SCENE 3: THE STABLE

JOSEPH:
>Now, Lord, this sound that I do hear,
>With this great solemnity,
>It gives my old heart much cheer,
>I hope glad tidings shortly to hear.

(JOSEPH *draws a curtain to reveal* MARY *and the
baby Jesus in the stable*)

MARY:

> Ah Joseph, my husband, come hither now,
> My child is born who is king of bliss.

JOSEPH:

> Now welcome to me, Maker of Man,
> With all the homage that I can.
> Your sweet mother here will I kiss.

MARY:

> Joseph, my husband, my child grows cold
> And we have no fire to keep Him warm.

(JOSEPH *takes the baby in his arms*)

JOSEPH:

> Now in my arms I shall Him fold,
> King of Kings, by field and farm,
> He might have had better than a manger old,
> And the breathing of beasts to make Him warm.

MARY:

> Now, Joseph, fetch hither my child,
> The Maker of Man, and high king of bliss.

(*She takes the baby from him and cradles it in her arms.* THE SHEPHERDS *come into the stable*)

SHEPHERD I:

> Hail, maid, mother and wife so mild!
> As the angel said, so have we found.
> I have no gift to present to this child
> But my pipe. Hold, hold, take it in your hand.
> The pipe in which much pleasure have I found.
> And now to honour your glorious birth,
> You shall have it to make you mirth.

SHEPHERD II:

> Now hail to you, child, and to your dame!
> For in a poor lodging here are you laid.

9

So the angel said, and told us your name.
Hold! Take my hat upon your head,
And now of one thing you are well sped.
Of weather you have no need to complain,
Of wind, nor sun, hail, snow nor rain.

SHEPHERD III:

Hail to you, Lord over water and lands!
For your coming we all make mirth.
Have here my mittens to put on your hands,
Other treasures have I none to present you with.

MARY:

Now herdsmen kind,
For your coming
To my child will I pray,
As he is Heaven's King,
To grant you His blessing.
The way to His bliss you may find
At your last day.

(SHEPHERDS *exit happily. The curtain is drawn on
the stable*)

## *SCENE 4: A STREET*

*A small* CROWD *that includes a* PROPHET *and* TWO
WOMEN. *The* FIRST SHEPHERD *comes running in
excitedly*

SHEPHERD I:

News, news
Of wonderful marvels
Strange to the ears!
Yet as scripture tells.

PROPHET:

Now truly, sir, I desire to know,

If it would please you for to show,
Of what manner of thing.

SHEPHERD I:
Very mystical unto your hearing —
Of the nativity of a king.

WOMAN I:
Of a king? Whence should he come?

SHEPHERD I:
From that royal region and mighty mansion,
The said celestial and heavenly wisdom.
The Second Person and God's own son,
For our sake is man become.
This godly spear
Descended here
Into a virgin clear,
She undefiled.

WOMAN II:
Why, has she a child?

SHEPHERD I:
Trust it well
And nevertheless
Is she a maid, even as she was,
And her son the King of Israel.

PROPHET:
I believe it perfectly
That unto the Deity
Nothing impossible may be;
Even though this work
Unto me is dark,
And a wondrous mystery.
But let me now hark.
Of what noble and high lineage is she
Who might this true Prince's mother be?

11

SHEPHERD I:

>Undoubtedly, she has come of high family,
>Of the house of David and Solomon the sage;
>And one of the same line joined to her by marriage.
>Of whose tribe
>We do subscribe
>This child's lineage.

WOMAN I:

>And why in that wise?

SHEPHERD I:

>It was the custom always
>To count the parent on the man's line,
>And not on the feminine,
>Among us here in Israel.

WOMAN II:

>I still can not see in any way
>How this child should be born without nature's
>    prejudice.

SHEPHERD I:

>No! No prejudice to nature, I dare well say.
>For the king of nature may
>Have all at His own wish.
>Did not the power of God
>Make Aaron's rod
>Bear fruit in one day?

PROPHET:

>True it is indeed.
>Yet I do marvel
>In what palace or castle
>You did Him see.

SHEPHERD I:

>Neither in halls, nor yet in bowers,
>Born would He not be,

Neither in castles, nor yet in towers
That beautiful were to see.
But at His Father's will,
The prophecy to fulfil,
Jesus, this king, born He was
To bring us unto Heaven!

*(Exit)*

## SCENE 5: OUTSIDE HEROD'S PALACE

*Fanfares. The* HERALD *enters*

HERALD:

Peace, lords, barons of great renown!
Peace, councillors, knights of noble power!
Peace, gentlemen, companions of orders small and
    great.
I command you to preserve complete silence!
Peace while your noble king is present here.
King Herod the Great . . . may the devil take you!

*(Fanfares as* HEROD, *superbly dressed, makes an
impressive entry with his* COURT)

HEROD:

I rule in Judah, the King of Israel,
And the mightiest conqueror that ever walked on
    ground,
For I am even he that made both heaven and hell,
And with my mighty power hold up this world
    round.
Both Magog and Madroc I did confound,
And with this bright sword cut their bones asunder,
So that all the wide world at my strokes did wonder.
I am the cause of this great light and thunder,
It is through my fury that such light is made.
The clouds my fearful countenance does so en-
    cumber

13

That often for fear of it the very earth does quake.
Look! When I with malice this bright sword take!
All the whole world from north to south
I may destroy with one word of my mouth.
Behold my countenance and my splendour
Brighter than the sun in the middle of the day.
Where can you have a greater succour
Than to behold my person in gorgeous array?
He who had the grace always on me to think,
Might live forever without either meat or drink.
And thus my triumphant fame most mighty does
    abound
Throughout this world in every region round.
And therefore, my herald here, called Calcas,
Warn every port that no ships must arrive,
Nor any stranger through my realms must pass,
Unless they pay for safe passage marks five.
Now speed you forth hastily,
For they that will the contrary,
Upon a gallows hanged shall be,
And, by Mahomet, get no grace of me!

HERALD:

Now lord and master, I leave you fast,
Thy worthy will, it shall be wrought.
And thy royal countries shall be passed
In as short a time as can be thought.

(*Exit* HERALD *at speed*)

HEROD:

Now shall our regions throughout be sought,
In every place, both east and west,
If any aliens to me are brought,
It shall not be in their best interest!
And now, while I take my rest,
Trumpets and viols and other harmony
Shall bless the waking of my majesty.

(*Music as* HEROD *and his* COURT *exit*)

## SCENE 6: A ROAD

*The* FIRST KING *enters. He looks up*

KING I:

Now blessed be God for His sweet sign,
For yonder a fair bright star I see!
He is come among us at this time,
As the prophets said it should be.

(*He kneels in prayer. The* SECOND KING *enters
some distance away, lost*)

KING II:

Out of my way I think I am,
For landmarks nowhere can I see,
Now God who on this earth made men
Send me some knowledge of where I may be.

(*As the* FIRST KING *gets up from prayer, he is seen
by the* SECOND KING *who approaches him*)

Speak, I pray you, noble king,
Where is your journey today?

KING I:

To seek a child is my intention,
Of whom the prophets have all made mention.
The time is come, now He is sent,
By yonder star there may you see.

KING II:

Sir, I pray you will consent
That I may ride with you to His presence.
To Him I will offer frankincense,
For the head of the whole church shall He be.

(*The* THIRD KING *enters and sees them*)

15

KING III:

    Hail kings, noble and true!

    Good sirs, where are you bound, I pray you?

KING I:

    To seek a child is our intent

    Which yonder star betokens, as you can see.

KING II:

    I purpose to give Him this present.

KING III:

    Sirs, I pray you, and that most humbly,

    That I may ride with you in company.

ALL:

    To Almighty God, we pray all three,

    That His precious person we may see.

*(Exeunt)*

## SCENE 7: HEROD'S COURT

*Fanfares as* HEROD *and his* COURT *enter. The* HERALD *rushes in and bows*

HERALD:

    Hail, lord! Greatest in might!

    Your commandment is right,

    Into your lands are come tonight

    Three kings and with them a great company.

HEROD:

    What is their errand in this country?

HERALD:

    To seek a king and a child, they say.

HEROD:

    Of what age would he be?

16

HERALD:
Only twelve days old.

HEROD:
And was he born so recently?

HERALD:
This is what I have been told.

HEROD:
Now, on pain of death, bring them before me;
And therefore, herald, travel in haste,
With all the speed that you can afford,
Before these kings have left the place.
See you bring all three before our court.

(HERALD *is about to leave but* HEROD *detains him*)

HEROD:
And in Jerusalem enquire more of that child,
But I warn you that your words must be mild,
For you must be careful and your craft conceal —
Destroy his power, those three kings beguile!

(*The* HERALD *bows and leaves. He meets the* THREE
KINGS *and hails them*)

HERALD:
Hail, lord kings, in your high degree!
Herod the king of this widespread state,
Desires to speak with you all three,
And your coming he does await.

KING I:
Sir, we are obedient to his will.
Brother, hurry to that lord's place;
We should be glad to speak our fill.
That child whom we seek, may He grant you His
grace!

*(The* HERALD *conducts them to Herod's court.*
*They bow before* HEROD*)*

HEROD:

Now welcome, lord kings; but do not fear
My bright array. Grovel not here.
Sirs, kings, as I understand,
A star has guided you into my hand,
In which you find great woe is planned,
By reason of its beams so bright.
Therefore, I pray you earnestly
That you certify the truth to me,
How long is it certainly
Since of that star you had first sight?

KING I:

Sir King, as I can truly say,
And will now show you, as is best,
Today is even the twelfth day
Since it appeared to us in the west.

HEROD:

Brothers, then there is no more to say,
But with heart and mind continue on your way,
And coming home, visit me, I say,
That I may know your news.
You shall revel in my country,
And in great concord banquet with me,
And that child then I myself will see
To honour his name.

*(The* KINGS *converse briefly then nod in agreement)*

KING I:

Now farewell, king of high degree,
We humbly take our leave of thee.

HEROD:

Then adieu, sirs, kings all three,

And while I live with me be bold,
For there is nothing in this country
But you shall have it for to hold.

(*The* KINGS *bow and go out.* HEROD'S *manner changes at once*)

HEROD:

Now these three kings have gone on their way,
Unwise and unwitting they have all sought;
When they come again, they shall die the same day,
And thus these vile wretches to death shall be
    brought.
Such is my pleasure!
He that against my laws will hold,
Be he Caesar or be he king,
I shall cast him into cares all cold,
And to death I shall them bring.

(*Exeunt*)

## SCENE 8: THE STABLE

*The curtain is drawn to reveal* JOSEPH, MARY *and the baby Jesus. The* THREE KINGS *present their gifts*

KING I:

Hail, Lord, who all this world has wrought!
Hail, God and man together!
For you have made all things of nought,
Although you lie poorly here;
A cup full of gold have I brought,
As a token that you have no peer.

KING II:

Hail to you, lord of magnificence!
As a token of priesthood and dignity high,
To you I present a cup full of incense
For it is fitting to have such sacrifice.

19

KING III:

> Hail to you, Lord, so looked for!
> I have brought you myrrh for mortality,
> As a sign that you shall raise man once more
> To life, by your death upon a tree.

MARY:

> Kings, God have mercy on your goodness,
> By the guidance of the god-head, here were you
>     sent.
> Your ways home the power of my sweet son will
>     bless,
> And in spirit reward you for your presents.

(*The* KINGS *leave the stable which is covered by the
curtain. They make a short journey then stop*)

KING I:

> Lord kings, considering our promise,
> Home to Herod we needs must go.

KING II:

> Now truly, brother, we can do no less.
> But I have travelled so long I know not what to do.

KING III:

> So have I, too; wherefore I pray,
> Let us all rest awhile on the ground.

KING I:

> Brother, I agree heartily with what you say,
> The grace of that dear child keep us all safe and
>     sound!

(*They lie down and go to sleep. An* ANGEL *appears*)

ANGEL:

> King of Tarshish, King Caspar,
> King of Arabia, Balthazar,

Melchior, King of Aginar!
To you I am now sent.
For fear of Herod go westwards home,
The Holy Ghost this knowledge has sent.

(*The* ANGEL *disappears. The* KINGS *awake*)

KING I:

Awake, lordings, I pray you awake!
For the voice of an angel I heard in my dream.

KING II:

That is quite true, what you do say,
For he called us plainly by our names.

KING III:

He ordered that we should go to the west,
For fear of Herod's false betrayal.

KING I:

And to do that, it will be best,
The child we have sought, show us the way!

KING III:

Since we needfully must go,
For fear of Herod who is so wroth,
Now farewell, brother, and brother also,
I here take my leave of you both.
We part this day.

ALL:

Now He that made us meet on the plain
And come to Mary, after her pain,
Give us grace in Heaven again
All to meet, I pray.

(*Exeunt*)

## SCENE 9: HEROD'S COURT

*Fanfares.* HEROD *enters with his* COURT

HERALD:

Hail, King, the worthiest indeed!
Hail, champion of chivalry throughout the wide
world!
Hail, the most mighty that ever bestrode a steed!
Hail, the most manly of men ever to meet foe in
armour!
Hail in thy honour!
These three kings who forth were sent,
And should have come again before your presence,
Lord, another way home they went,
Contrary to their promise.

HEROD:

Another way! Out! Out! Out!
Have those false traitors done these things?
I stamp! I stare! I glare all about!
If I should take them, I should burn them to cinders!
I rage — I rave — and now I run mad!
Oh that these villains should spoil what I planned!
They shall be hanged if I find them out!

(*He rages about his Court then faces his soldiers*)

And that wretch of Bethlehem, he shall die,
And thus I shall destroy his prophecy.
How say you, my knights, is this not good advice?
That all young children for this shall die,
To be slain by the sword?
Then I, Herod, will live in fame,
And everyone shall dread my name,
And offer me gold, riches and grain.
Would this not pleasure afford?

22

SOLDIER I:

My lord, King Herod by name,
Your words against my will they be.
To see so many children die would be a shame,
Therefore you get no support from me.

SOLDIER II:

Well said, fellow, I side with you.
Lord king, you may quite well see,
So great a murder of children is cruel
And will cause a rising in your country.

HEROD:

A rising! Out! Out! Out!
Out, villainous wretches! Death on you, I cry!
Look that my will is utterly wrought,
Or upon a gallows you both shall die.

SOLDIER I:

Now, cruel Herod, we shall perform this deed,
Your will in this realm, it must be obeyed.
All children of that age, they must lie dead,
Now with all my strength they shall be slayed.

SOLDIER II:

And I will swear here upon your bright sword,
All the children I find, killed shall be.
It will make many a mother weep and be afraid,
When in our bright armour they shall us see.

HEROD:

Now you have sworn, away you go
And work my will both by day and night,
Then will I joyfully trip like a doe.
But when they are dead — I warn you — bring
    them into my sight!

(*Exeunt*)

23

## SCENE 10: THE STABLE

MARY, JOSEPH *and the baby asleep. An* ANGEL *appears.*

ANGEL:
> Mary and Joseph, to you I say,
> Sweet word from the Father I bring you aright.
> Out of Bethlehem into Egypt go your way,
> And with you take the king, full of might,
> For fear of Herod's sway.

(*The* ANGEL *disappears.* JOSEPH *wakes*)

JOSEPH:
> Arise up, Mary, quickly and soon,
> Our Lord's will must be done,
> As the Angel bade us.

MARY:
> Meekly, Joseph, my own spouse,
> Towards that country let us repair,
> In Egypt to some sort of house,
> God grant us His grace safe to come there!

(*She takes up the baby and they go out*)


## SCENE 11: A STREET

THREE WOMEN *enter with babies in their arms. The* WOMEN *sing the Coventry Carol*

WOMEN:
> O sisters two
> How may we do
> For to preserve this day,
> This poor young thing
> For whom we sing
> By, by, lully, lullay.

*Chorus*
Lully, lullay, thou little tiny child,
By, by, lully lullay, thou little tiny child,
By, by, lully, lullay.

Herod the king
In his raging
Charged he hath this day
His men of might
In his own sight
All young children to slay.

*Chorus*

That woe is me
Poor child for this
And ever mourn and may
For thy parting
Neither say nor sing,
By, by, lully, lullay.

*Chorus*

WOMAN I:
I lull my child so wondrous sweet,
And in my arms I do it keep
So that it shall not cry.

WOMAN II:
That babe that is born in Bethlehem, so meek,
O save my child and me from villainy!

WOMAN III:
Be still, be still, my little tiny child!
That lord of lords save both thee and me!
For Herod has sworn with words so wild
That all young children slain shall be.

(SOLDIERS *enter with drawn swords. The* WOMEN
*try to run out but the* SOLDIERS *block their way*)

25

SOLDIER I:

    Say now, withered wives, why hurry away?
    What you bear in your arms we needs must see.
    If your children be boys, they will die this day,
    For at Herod's command, all things must be.

SOLDIER II:

    If I once seize them in my hands,
    I will not spare to slay them so.
    We must fulfil Herod's commands,
    Or else be traitors, condemned to woe.

WOMAN I:

    Sir knights, pray of your courtesy,
    Today shame not your chivalry
    But on my child have pity!

WOMAN II:

    See you false and filthy cur!
    A blow will you be given here.
    I will spare no cost.

*(The* SOLDIERS *drive the* WOMEN *out and kill the babies offstage. Loud wailing from the* WOMEN. *The* SOLDIERS *enter with arms and swords covered in blood.)*

SOLDIER I:

    Who has ever heard such cries
    From mothers who have their children lost?
    All greatly cursing our villainies
    Throughout the realm in every coast,
    For which men's lives are like to be lost.
    For this great crime that here is done,
    I fear a great revenge will come.

SOLDIER II:

    O Brother, such things we must not name,
    Therefore to Herod let us go,

For he it is must bear the blame,
He was the cause we acted so.
They must all be brought to him, you know,
With wains and wagons piled up high.
I fear it will be a woeful sight.

(*A fanfare.* HEROD *sweeps in. They go to him*)

SOLDIER II:
Hail, Herod, King! You soon may see
How many thousands have been slain.

(*The* WOMEN *rush in, their babies dripping with blood*)

WOMAN I:
Herod, king, this I tell you!
All your deeds have come to nought!

WOMAN II:
This child is gone into Egypt to dwell.
See, sir, in your own land what wonders are
  wrought!

(*The* WOMEN *rush out*)

HEROD:
Into Egypt! Alas! What woe!
Here in my land no more can I bide.
Saddle my horse! For in haste I will go,
After those traitors now I shall ride.
They shall be slain!
Now all men come fast
Into Egypt in haste!
All that country will I lay waste
Till I have found them.

(*He rushes out. The* TWO SOLDIERS *remain*)

*END OF THE PAGEANT OF THE SHEARMEN
AND TAYLORS*

## THE WEAVERS' PAGEANT

*The action continues with the* TWO SOLDIERS
*addressing the audience*

SOLDIER I:
> Look, friends, thus may you see
> How God is always working in man.
> Now all we that His servants be
> Have great cause to rejoice in Him.

SOLDIER II:
> Therefore here I exhort you all
> That in this place assembled be,
> Unto this child for mercy call,
> Who shall redeem us upon a tree.
> And that glorious bliss that we may see,
> Which He has ordained for all men,
> In His celestial place to be

BOTH:
> IN SECULA SECULORUM, AMEN!

*(Exeunt)*

## *SCENE 12: THE TEMPLE*

SIMEON, *very old, enters and prays*

SIMEON:
> O lord of lords, with all my heart I beseech thee,
> Of your infinite work to send me the true light
> Clearly to expound this same holy prophecy.
> And also of that king I may have a sight,
> Who by redemption will us all release.

(ANNA, *the ancient prophetess, enters*)

ANNA:

O sovereign Simeon!
If I might live until that day,
The holy of holiest to see
I would have that joy for which I pray.
God grant me grace that this may be.

SIMEON:

Now Anna, sister and dear friend,
Let us both with a holy intent
In this true faith our lives end,
Praising that Lord who is omnipotent.
Therefore I think it very expedient,
In continual prayer to endure,
So that we may know His gracious pleasure.

ANNA:

O sovereign Simeon! This famous counsel
Greatly gladdens my heart.
Nothing contents my mind so well.
Therefore at this time I will depart.

(*Exit*)

SIMEON:

Friends, now it is time to pray
Before I take my rest.
Now, Lord, who made all things of nought,
Both heaven and hell and every creature,
As you know my inner thought,
Strengthen me when it is your pleasure.
For I do covet no more treasure
Than the time of your Nativity
With my mortal eyes to see.
I commit my works with all circumstance
Wholly unto your law and ordinance.

(SIMEON *settles down to rest. An* ANGEL *appears*)

ANGEL:
>Simeon, that Lord in Trinity
>Whom you have always desired to see,
>At your temple offered will be
>Into your hands this same day.
>Therefore make speed in every way
>So that the temple in order may be
>To receive this Prince with all humility.

(*The* ANGEL *disappears.* SIMEON *gets up*)

SIMEON:
>O lord of lords, thanks be to thee!
>These glorious tidings that here are told
>In my heart so gladden me
>That I am lighter a thousandfold
>Than ever I was before.

(*His* CLERKS *enter*)

>Now friends all, be of good cheer,
>And to our temple draw we near,
>Such wondrous news I do hear.
>That babe is born in dignity
>Whom we so long have desired to see,
>Our Lord and King almighty.

CLERK:
>Now blessed must that Lord be
>That day and hour we shall see
>His glorious person in Trinity.

SIMEON:
>No longer, sirs, let us abide,
>But to the temple with all speed
>To receive the saviour of this world wide,
>And him serve with love and dread.

CLERK:

> To serve a Prince of such magnificence,
> Sir, I humbly ask of you,
> Since you have wisdom and intelligence,
> Instruct me, sir, what I must do.

SIMEON:

> Since you seek instruction from me,
> I think better of your wits, truly.
> With hearts both humble and meek
> One of us must hold the light
> And the other the sacrifice.
> And I, on my knees, as it is right
> The office will exercise
> Unto that babe so sweet.

CLERK:

> Then must we this altar array
> And clothes of honour upon it lay,
> And the ground strew with flowers gay
> That of sweet odour smell.

SIMEON:

> And when he approaches near this place,
> Sing we then with cheerful voice,
> And ring the bells for joy.

SIMEON/CLERKS (*singing*):

> Rejoice, rejoice, all that here be!
> The Angel these tidings has brought,
> That Simeon before he die,
> Shall see the Lord who all has wrought.
>
> Wherefore now let us all prepare,
> Our temple must in order be,
> For He has put away our care,
> The Second Person in Trinity.

(*Exeunt*)

## SCENE 13:  A HOUSE

MARY *rocks the baby in a crib*. ANGEL GABRIEL *appears unto her*

GABRIEL:
> Hail, Mary, meek and mild!
> The virtue in you shall never fade.
> Hail, maiden, and your child,
> Who all this world has made!
> With your son, our heavenly king,
> Unto the temple you should go.
> Take two white turtle doves with you also,
> Present them with the child in offering.
> Tarry not, you must soon be gone,
> And leave not Joseph behind at home.
> Bid your husband to make all haste,
> To guide you hither to that place.
> For rest you well, Mary, with much solace,
> For now I must depart.

(ANGEL GABRIEL *disappears*)

MARY:
> O Lord of Lords, be our guide
> Wherever we walk in this country wide,
> And these two doves for us provide
> So them we shall not miss.

(JOSEPH *enters*)

> Now welcome, my spouse so free!

JOSEPH:
> Rest well, Mary! What say you now?

MARY:
> Sweet news, husband, I bring to you.
> The Angel of the Lord has been with me
> To give us both a warning

That you and I with holy intent,
After the law, our child should present
In Jerusalem, there to make offering.

JOSEPH:

Now Mary, whom I will never deny,
I am ready at all times, standing by.

MARY:

Thank you, husband, who speaks so gently.
Look now, Joseph, see if you can spy
Two turtle doves and bring them to me.
This offering suits our degree.

JOSEPH:

No, no Mary, it cannot be,
Mine age is such I can hardly see.

MARY:

Sweet Joseph, fulfil our Lord's behest.

JOSEPH:

Why, and would you have me hunt birds' nests?
I pray you, dame, leave off these jests.
For, wife, I will never waste my wits,
Waiting and watching where the woodcock sits.
Now I am old and no longer sound,
The smallest twig could trip me to the ground.

MARY:

Truly, Joseph, do not fear,
Our Lord will help you with your task here.

JOSEPH:

Eh? What? Eh? God help us all!
Your memory must be wondrous small,
On me so rudely to call.
You think nothing of my age.
The weakest goes ever to the wall!
Therefore, go yourself, or get a new page.

MARY:

> Husband, this is no woman's deed,
> Therefore, Joseph, your help I need.
> There is no other way.

JOSEPH:

> How say all this company,
> Who be wedded the same as me?
> I think that you suffer much woe.
> For he who marries a young thing,
> Must always do her every bidding,
> Or else his hands he may wring,
> And that you all do know.

MARY:

> Why say you so, sir? You are to blame.

JOSEPH:

> Dame, all this company will say the same.
> Is it not so? — Speak, men! For shame!
> Tell the truth as well as you can.
> They who will not their wives please
> Suffer often pain and dis-ease,
> The only man who gets some peace
> Is he who has to do with none.

MARY:

> Leave off these jests, for my love,
> And go for those fowls, sir, I pray.
> The father in heaven that is above
> Will speed you on your journey.

JOSEPH:

> Then I will go by and by,
> Though it can not be hastily.
> With all my heart I will go and spy
> If any fowls be in my way.
> I will find them if I may
> Before I finish my journey.

(*He sets out on a short journey and is soon tired. He stops to rest*)

I wander about myself alone
Yet I can see no turtle dove.
Lord in heaven, your help send down!
Find me these fowls to please my love.

(*The* ANGEL GABRIEL *appears and puts two caged doves into his hands.* JOSEPH *is amazed*)

GABRIEL:
Arise, Joseph, and take no thought
For these birds that you have sought.
Even to your hand I have them brought,
And therefore be of good cheer.
Tarry no longer here.

(ANGEL GABRIEL *disappears*)

JOSEPH:
O praise be unto that Lord so excellent
That these two fowls to me has sent.

(*He hurries back to* MARY)

Now rest well, Mary, my own darling.
Look, dame, I have done your bidding,
And brought these doves for our offering.
Here they are — both alive.

MARY:
Now the Father in heaven that is above
Bless you, Joseph, for this deed!
Further, I pray you, for my love,
Unto the temple let us speed.

JOSEPH:
Eh? Blow a while, dame, I say!
I have laboured all this day.

35

After my journey I must now rest,
Therefore go yourself, Mary, if you think it best.

MARY:
No, sweet husband, you well know
To go alone is not for me.
Therefore, good sir, I pray you so
That I should have your company.

JOSEPH:
Look, friends, here you may know
The manner of my wife is this.
To Jerusalem with her I must go
Whether or not I wish.
Now is this not a burdensome life?
Look, sirs, what it is to have a wife.
Take up your child, Mary, I say,
And let us walk easily on the way.

(*He gathers a few things for the journey. She picks up the baby*)

MARY:
We shall be there when God wills it to be,
Set forward, husband, and let us see.

(*Exeunt*)


## SCENE 14: THE TEMPLE

SIMEON *is sleeping. An* ANGEL *appears*

ANGEL:
Awake, Simeon, fear you nought,
In all the haste that ever may be,
Receive that lord who has all wrought,
And with him his mother, Mary.

(ANGEL *disappears.* SIMEON *prays*)

SIMEON:

> I thank you, lord and king of might,
> Though all my strength through age has gone,
> That I shall see this glorious sight.
> Blessed be the hour that you were born!

(*He gets up*)

> Now to receive this king of peace,
> That out of danger will us release,
> Our high merits shall he increase,
> In joy abundantly.

(*He calls to the* CLERKS *who enter at once*)

> Now, clerks, come forth and do your office,
> This altar hastily you must array,
> For here will be the most solemn sacrifice.
> Put everything in order, my friends.

(*The* CLERKS *quickly prepare the altar*)

CLERK:

> Look, master, now both man and place
> Be all ready at your bidding.

SIMEON:

> Then, sirs, you must come forth apace.
> Merrily let the bells ring!

(*The bells ring.* ANNA *enters*)

> Anna, sister, go you with me,
> Now to receive the prince of honour,
> And him to welcome reverently
> As of this world, lord and governor.

ANNA:

> Now father Simeon, I am obedient
> And your gracious pleasure will obey.
> To serve the lord who is omnipotent,
> Let us go meet him on the way.

*(They move to meet* JOSEPH *and* MARY *who enter with the baby Jesus and the doves.* A CLERK *takes the doves)*

MARY:

    Hail, sovereign Simeon so good!
    My beautiful son here I bring to thee,
    To offer him up in flesh and blood,
    As by the law he ought to be.

SIMEON:

    Now holy Mary and Joseph, too,
    You are most welcome to this place,
    God above has blessed both of you,
    And grounded you now in His grace.

JOSEPH:

    Now gentle bishop, Simeon, I pray,
    The honest truth you must now tell.
    Is not this as pretty a boy
    As you have ever known?
    This little child I love so well
    As though he were mine own.

MARY:

    Receive him, Simeon, with all cheer.
    Into your hands take him here.

*(She hands the baby Jesus to* SIMEON*)*

SIMEON:

    Welcome, our joy! Welcome, our mirth!
    Welcome to us, that heavenly flower.
    Now blessed be the day and hour
    Of thy glorious birth.

ANNA:

    Now welcome, king of kings all!
    Now welcome, maker of mankind!

Welcome to us both great and small,
Good Lord, your servants now have in mind.

SIMEON:

On, on with me, my friends dear,
With this child that we have here.

(*They move in procession to the altar.* SIMEON *and
the* CLERKS *sing*)

ALL:

Behold now it is come to pass
That many years before was told,
How that Christ, our true Messiah,
By Judas should be bought and sold.

For our offence he man became
His father's wrath to pacify
And after meekly as a lamb,
Upon the cross there did he die.

O Lord as though hast redeemed us all,
And suffered at Mount Calvary,
Strengthen us both great and small,
That in thy truth we live and die.

(*During the song,* SIMEON *reaches the altar with the
baby and completes the ceremony of purification.
The* CLERK *who holds the doves stands beside him*)

SIMEON:

Now you are come, Lord, to my hand.
Forgive me that so unworthy I am.

(*He hands the baby to* MARY. *She and* JOSEPH *leave*)

Look, friends, how God for us has wrought!
Blessed must He be in word and thought!
I was lame of foot and hand,
Yet now am old as you can see.
I thank the Lord for this sign,
And ever will His servant be.

SIMEON/CLERKS:

> Of our mistakes may He amend us!
> From our follies may He defend us!
> And to His high throne may He send us!
> IN SECULA SECULORUM, AMEN!

(Exeunt)

## SCENE 15: NAZARETH

JOSEPH *addresses the audience*

JOSEPH:

> Good friends, I pray you, now come with me
> And lend your hearts to our device.
> For we must all make a journey
> Across twelve long years — in a trice.
> This holy child that brought such joy,
> Throughout this time grew straight and true.
> Our precious babe is now a boy.
> See Jesus Christ come into view!

(MARY *enters with the boy* JESUS, *who is carving
a piece of wood. He is twelve years old*)

MARY:

> I thank the Lord omnipotent,
> It does me good my son to see.
> Therefore, Joseph, I wish he went
> Unto Jerusalem with you and me.
> For now some twelve years old is he,
> And much desires some company.

JOSEPH:

> Now, dame, he is a pretty page,
> And, as you say, so well come on
> He has no equal of his own age.
> I pray God makes him a right good man.

MARY:

> Now Jesus, my son, that I love so dear,
> What mirth do you make, child, this day?

JESUS:

> I thank you, mother, in every way,
> And at your hand I am here
> To do your service both night and day,
> And ready always to bring you cheer.

JOSEPH:

> Come, my son, a blessing on thee!
> You shall to Jerusalem with your mother and me.
> Some goodly sights you will see
> Upon this our festival day.

JESUS:

> Now come on, mother, and fear you nought.
> Begin your journey, as you ought,
> The Father in Heaven that all has wrought,
> May He keep you from distress!

JOSEPH:

> Now this is wittily said and well,
> Good Lord! When I to mind do call
> The time on earth when I was small,
> Many winters gone —
> Lord God, benedicite!
> Children now much wiser be
> Than was an old man then.

(*They set out on a journey and reach the Temple*)

MARY:

> Come on, Joseph, gentle husband,
> The place is even here at hand.
> Good company we there may find.

JOSEPH:

> Eh! Eh! Dame, in faith I can walk no more!

41

My legs are weary, my feet are sore,
I must needs come behind.

*(They go up to the altar,* JESUS *first, and sing an
anthem.* JOSEPH *and* MARY *come down.* JESUS
*stays at the altar, fascinated by what he sees)*

Now Mary, my wife, come hither to me.
All things are done as they should be,
And service sung full solemnly
For this our festival day.

MARY:
Now, husband, then let us three
Make all haste that ever may be,
Home to go with company
To bring us on our way.

*(They set off but* JESUS *is distracted and steals away.
They do not notice his absence)*

JOSEPH:
Mary, my spirits have been washed clean,
And cast right out is every woe,
With these solemn sights that we have seen,
In yonder temple that we went to.

MARY:
Truly, Joseph, it gives me great joy,
That we to Jerusalem have been.
And taken with us our dear boy,
Who these solemn sights has seen.

JOSEPH:
Then homeward, Mary, on our way
While we still have light of day.

*(They journey a while then she misses Jesus)*

MARY:

Alas, Joseph! My son I can nowhere find!
Most certainly, sir, we have left our child behind.

JOSEPH:

What? Mary, I say, be of good cheer,
He has only done what others do.
Children together will always draw near.
Jesus, I promise you, will overtake us soon.

MARY:

It helps me not, Joseph, such words to hear,
My child is gone and I do fear!
Of sorrow now shall be my song
Until I see my son again.

JOSEPH:

Dame, of his welfare I would be glad.
God preserve him from any woe!
Therefore, Mary, be no longer sad,
But again to the temple let us go.

(*Exeunt*)


## SCENE 16: THE TEMPLE

THREE DOCTORS *enter with large law books*

DOCTOR III:

Now all good people, draw you near,
And in this place give your attendance.
How you should live, here you may learn,
According to your allegiance.
For it is well-known unto this presence
That doctors we are and of high degree,
And have the laws in custody.

(JESUS *enters*)

JESUS:

> Lords, much love be with you now
> And peace among this company!

DOCTOR III:

> Son, away you must needs go,
> For other business in hand have we.

DOCTOR II:

> We have important things to do
> And will not be bothered with thee.

DOCTOR I:

> Good son, you are too young to learn
> The high mystery of Moses' law.
> Your reason can not yet discern,
> For your wit is not worth a straw.

JESUS:

> Now, kind sirs, say what you may,
> I need to learn nothing of you.

DOCTOR II:

> This little child with busy tongue
> All secrets clearly he thinks he knows.

DOCTOR III:

> Now certainly, son, you are too young
> By knowledge clear to know our laws.

JESUS:

> You doctors all that be present,
> I pray you, wonder no more at me.
> For of your laws the whole intent
> I know as well as any of thee.
> For in those places have I been
> Where all our laws were first wrought.

DOCTOR I:

> Now sit you here and it shall be seen
> For certain now if you know ought.

(JESUS *sits among them*)

Is it not a wondrous sight
That a child our reasons should teach?

JESUS:
Sirs, the Holy Ghost in me did light,
So my power is to preach;
And of the God-head, most of might,
Perfectly here I may teach.

DOCTOR III:
Whence came this child, I marvel so,
That speaks to us mystically?

JESUS:
Sirs, I came all you before,
And after you again shall be.

DOCTOR II:
Masters all, what may this mean?
I wonder how this can be.
So young a child I have not seen
Talking with clerks so cunningly.

JESUS:
Sirs, I will show you by authors evident,
Higher mysteries than ever you read or saw.

DOCTOR I:
Say, son, which was the First Commandment
That was set down in Moses' law?

JESUS:
Since your books are laid open here,
Set forth your reasons and do not forbear.

DOCTOR II:
First, honour God above all other
With all your heart and all your will.

And as yourself, love your neighbour,
And in no way do him ill.

DOCTOR III:
Since these two, son, we have showed,
Tell us the other commandments, pray.

JESUS:
The third bids you in every way
From your labour you should rest,
And truly keep the Sabbath day,
Yourself, your servant and your beast.

The fourth bids you to do your best,
Your mother and father to honour;
And when their goods become decreased,
With all your might you must them succour.

The fifth commandment forbids anger,
Man or woman you must not kill;
To flee adultery is another,
And all that teaches any ill.

The seventh says you should not steal
Your neighbours' goods, more nor less,
The eighth forbids you to counsel
Or to bear false witness.

The ninth forbids idols great,
To worship them you must not dare,
The last wishes that you should not covet
Your neighbours' goods, or him impair.

DOCTOR I:
Behold, how he does our law expound
Who never learned a book to read;
Than all of us he is much more profound
In all truths, if we take heed.

DOCTOR II:
Brothers, let him go his ways,

For if this is known, take my warning.
The people would give him more praise
Than we doctors for all our learning.

(JOSEPH *and* MARY *enter*)

MARY:

Ah, Joseph, I see what I have sought!
In this world there never was such a sight.
See, husband, where he sits aloft
Among those masters of so much might.

JOSEPH:

Now, Mary, wife, you know full well,
As I have told you many a time,
With men of might I dare not meddle,
Look, maid, how they sit in their clothes fine?

MARY:

If you will not the errand do,
No remedy then but that I must go.

(MARY *goes across to* JESUS)

Ah Jesus, Jesus, my son so sweet!
Your going from me so suddenly
Has caused us both to wail and weep
With bitter tears abundantly.

JESUS:

Mother, why did you seek me so?
It has often been said unto you
My Father's wish I must fulfil
In every point, for good or ill.

MARY:

Son, these words that you do tell,
As yet I can not understand,
But my heart, I know this well,
Is very glad that you are found.

JESUS:

Now farewell, masters of might and main,
For with my mother I must now go
To comfort her once again.
After three days' dread she has found me again.

DOCTOR II:

Now, son, whenever you come this way,
Be bold with us here, I pray,
And if to age live you may,
Your friends will be full glad.

MARY:

Now farewell, lords of high degree,
I take my leave of you all three.
That Lord that is in Trinity
May He keep you from all care!

JOSEPH:

Now farewell, friends all,
I must away, whatever befall,
Needs must that needs shall!
By me here may you know.
Ah, and may you use all your ways
At every time your wife to please,
You will then avoid dis-ease.
God grant that you may do so!

(JOSEPH, MARY *and* JESUS *go out. The* DOCTORS
*watch*)

DOCTOR II:

Surely it can no other way be,
For he is not living that ever did see
Such high learning and excellence
In so tender a youth.

DOCTOR III:

Is this not a wondrous case

48

That this young child such knowledge has?
Most surely he has a special grace
To utter so much truth.

DOCTOR I:
Now brothers both, by my counsel,
These mightly matters now set aside,
And to avoid more peril
That here may betide,
Let us therefore no longer abide
These causes to contend,
For the day is almost at an end.

*(They gather their books and move off)*

Now, friends, touching our festival day,
Is there anything else I should say?

DOCTOR II:
No more but even away
For the night draws fast upon.

DOCTOR III:
And of your company I would now pray,
And here I take my leave of every man.

*(Exeunt)*

## *END OF THE WEAVERS' PAGEANT*

## SCENE 17: THE BAPTISM

JOHN THE BAPTIST *stands ready to baptise the queue of men and women*

JOHN:

Almighty God and lord of all,
Most wonderful is man's unheeding,
For day by day I teach your law
And tell them, Lord, of your coming
Who all has wrought —
Men are so dull that my preaching
Is worth nought.
When I have, Lord, in thy name,
Baptised the folk in waters bright,
I have said that He will come
After me, who has more might
Than I or any on earth.
I am but a messenger of His glorious birth.
This place here that is so pleasing
The River Jordan is named.
Here is neither church nor building,
But where the Father will ordain,
There shall His will be done.

(*A line of people come to be baptised. He baptises a man and a woman*)

JOHN:

I baptise you here this day,
In nomine patris et filii
Et spiritus altissimi.

(JESUS *comes to be baptised.* JOHN *is in awe of him*)

JESUS:

John, God's servant, I come to you
To be baptised in waters clear;
My father, that to you is dear,

His word has sent me to fulfil;
Here I am and it is my will
That it should be so.

JOHN:

But baptism is taken, this I know,
To wash and cleanse man of his sin.
You need not under water go,
For, Lord, you have no stain.

JESUS:

Mankind may not unbaptised go.
Since men will me their mirror take,
I will therefore
Myself be baptised, for their sake.
And also know, that from this day
In this baptismal water will stay
My spirit evermore.
Come — baptise me, John, in this place.

JOHN:

Almighty God, great is your grace.
I am not worthy to do this deed.

(JESUS *smiles and waits to be baptised.* JOHN
*reaches out but his hands tremble*)

Now help me, Lord . . .

(ANGELS *sing 'Veni, creator spiritus'.* JOHN *baptises*
JESUS)

Jesus, my lord, in might the most,
I baptise you here this day,
In the name of the Father and of the Son,
And of the Holy Ghost.
Now, bless me, Lord, I pray.

JESUS:

I grant you, John, for your labour

Everlasting joy in bliss.
Now go you forth once more to preach
Against the people that do amiss.
And to all men the truth teach.
Farewell, John, I go my way.

(JESUS *leaves and* JOHN *watches him go*)

JOHN:

Farewell, sweet saviour of those forlorn.
Farewell, the steersman of those by storms and
    sorrows beset.
Farewell, redeemer of mankind's woe!
Great glory be with you wherever you go!
Farewell, my master, Lord and King,
Farewell my friend,
I follow you in everything,
Unto the end!

(*Exit*)


## SCENE 18: THE MINISTRY

CHELIDONIUS, *a blind boy, is led in by his* SISTER.
*Passers-by ignore his begging bowl*

CHELIDONIUS:

Your alms, good people, in charity,
For me that am blind and never did see,
Your neighbour born here in this city;
Help me, help me, before you go hence.

(JESUS *enters with his disciples,* JOHN, PETER *and*
JUDAS)

PETER:

Master, instruct us in what we find.
Why was this boy born blind?

JOHN:
> Was it for his sinful mind,
> Or did his parents offend?

JESUS:
> It was neither for his offence
> Nor the sins of his parents
> That he was born so blind.
> But for this cause especially,
> To display God's great glory,
> That His power may be made manifest
> In the bringing back of sight.

(JESUS *puts his hands over the boy's eyes and restores his sight.* JESUS *and the* DISCIPLES *leave*)

CHELIDONIUS:
> Praised be omnipotent God in His height! —
> I see all things in this light.
> Blessed be God forever!

(TWO NEIGHBOURS *enter*)

NEIGHBOUR I:
> Neighbour, if I should tell the truth,
> This surely is the very youth
> Who asked for alms yesterday —
> It is the very same.

NEIGHBOUR II:
> No, no, neighbour, it is not he,
> Though the likeness is great, I must agree.

CHELIDONIUS:
> Good friends, truly I am he
> That was blind. Now I see!
> I am no other, honestly.

NEIGHBOUR I:
> Then tell the truth, we pray you now,

When this happened — and also how
It is that you who yesterday
Could see no earthly thing,
Now see perfectly.

CHELIDONIUS:
The man whom they call Jesus,
Who works miracles daily with us,
And whom we find so gracious —
He touched my eyes.

NEIGHBOUR II:
Where is he now, I pray?

CHELIDONIUS:
I do not know.

NEIGHBOUR II:
You will come with us along the way,
And tell the Pharisees what you say.

(*They drag him before the* TWO PHARISEES *and*
TWO JEWS *who enter*)

Look here, Lords and judges of right!
We bring you a boy that had no sight,
And on the Sabbath through one man's might,
Was healed, restored and sees!

NEIGHBOUR I:
Declare to them, you wicked boy,
Who restored your sight to you.

CHELIDONIUS:
Jesus touched my eyes, I say.

PHARISEE I:
That man is not of God, I lay.
He violates the Sabbath day.
I judge him to be mad.

54

PHARISEE II:

> It can not enter into my mind
> That he who can cure this boy blind
> Should be a madman — I believe it not.
> Who is he that healed you?

CHELIDONIUS:

> He is a prophet of the Jews,
> And he restored to me my eyes.

PHARISEE I:

> Give praise to God, you crafty slave,
> Be sure that you no further rave,
> And say that Jesus saved you
> And gave you back your sight.

PHARISEE II:

> He is a sinner — that we know.
> Believe us, as is right.

CHELIDONIUS:

> If it be sinful, I do not know,
> But this is the truth I tell you now.
> When I was blind and in great woe
> He cured me, as you see.
> Come you now and follow him
> And have remission of all your sin.

PHARISEE I:

> Damn slave, take care how far you go!
> Would you have as disciples such as we?

PHARISEE II:

> No, no. Moses' disciples we all be,
> For God did speak with him.
> But whence this man is we can not know.

CHELIDONIUS:

> I marvel at this, at men like you,

That you know not whence he should be,
Who has given me sight that never did see —
Knowing this most certainly,
God hears not sinners.

PHARISEE I:

Miserable wretch, will you teach us,
Whose lives be more than virtuous,
Whom all the scriptures can discuss?
We spurn you from this place!

(*The* PHARISEES *exit. The* NEIGHBOURS *and*
JEWS *stalk* CHELIDONIUS *but* JESUS *enters with*
PETER *and* JOHN, *and speaks to the boy*)

JESUS:

Do you believe in God's son, truly?

CHELIDONIUS:

Yes, gracious Lord, but who is he?

JESUS:

You have seen him with your eye,
He is the man who talks with you now.

CHELIDONIUS:

Then I honour him with a free heart,
And shall serve him till from life I part.

(CHELIDONIUS *goes out with his* SISTER)

JEW I:

Tell us, man that makes such mystery,
Before you do our souls injury,
Tell us here straightforwardly —
Art thou Christ?

JESUS:

You believe not what you see,
And you would not join my flock.

56

Well I know them every one,
And for them I have ordained
Everlasting life.
No man shall take my sheep from me,
For my Father in majesty
Is greater than the greatest that be,
Or any that ever was.

JEW I:

You are a man as well as I,
Making yourself God here openly.
There thou liest foul and falsely,
Both in word and thought.

JEW II:

You shall not pass until all be denied.
Help, men, and gather stones
To beat him for his pride.
He scorns us! Break his bones!

JEW I:

One hit now, by this heavenly light,
And He *will* have a son on high!

(*They stone* JESUS *who backs away*)

JESUS:

Wretches all! Many a good deed
Have I done in your grave need —
This is how you repay me!

(JESUS *and* DISCIPLES *go out*)

JEW II:

Out, alas! Where is he gone?

JEW I:

I would have struck him with this stone.

JEW II:

He has fled away.

But never fear. Another day
His final hour will come.

*(The* JEWS *and* NEIGHBOURS *go out.* JESUS *enters with his* DISCIPLES)

PETER:

Master, the Jews will stone you again
If they see you here.

JESUS:

Peter, you do not seem to know
That there are twelve hours in the day,
And who in that time walks on his way
Trespasses not at all.
To the daylight liken me,
And to the twelve hours ye
That are well-lit through following me.
For I am the light of the world,
And he who follows me today,
May not go an evil way,
For light is his eternally.
Brethren, go we to Bethany.
Lazarus, my friend, is sleeping there.

JOHN:

Lord, if he is sleeping, he is safe,
For in his sleep no perils prey.
Therefore it is not good to waste
Your time and go that way.

JESUS:

Lazarus is dead — and thither will I.

PETER:

Let us follow him on his journey,
And die with him devotedly,
For no other way can it be.

*(They follow* JESUS *to the tomb of Lazarus, where* MARY OF BETHANY *sits and weeps)*

MARY:
> Master, Lazarus my brother is dead.

JESUS:
> Mary, you know that there is no death.
> They live who love me.

MARY:
> This I know.
> But, Lord, my sister laments his going.
> In sorrow and longing for him she weeps.

JESUS:
> Your brother Lazarus only sleeps.
> Bid Martha come to me.

*(*MARY *fetches* MARTHA *who is weeping)*

MARTHA:
> Ah Jesus! Had you been here,
> Lazarus my brother, my brother dear,
> Would not be dead.

JESUS:
> Martha, your brother shall rise, I say.

MARTHA:
> That I believe, Lord, in good faith,
> That he shall rise on the last day.
> Then hope I to see him.

JESUS:
> Martha, Martha, I say to you,
> I am the resurrection and the life.
> Whoso believes steadfastly
> In me, I tell you faithfully,
> Though he be dead and down does lie,
> Yet he will live and be mended.

MARTHA:
>Ah Lord, four days have passed away
>Since he was buried in his grave,
>And now his body fast decays.

JESUS:
>Martha, did I not say to thee
>That if you believed fully in me,
>The grace of God you soon would see?

(*He turns aside to pray*)

>Father in heaven, I thank thee
>That thou so soon hast heard me.
>Well I know and well believe
>Thou hearest my intent.
>But for these people who stand hereby
>I will speak more openly,
>That they may believe steadfastly
>That from thee I was sent . . .

(*He turns to the tomb*)

>Lazarus, come forth, I command thee!

(*They all watch the tomb.* LAZARUS *comes slowly forth then stops to address the audience*)

LAZARUS:
>Worms eat the dead — look!
>I am the mirror of decay.
>Let me be your book.
>Take your example from me,
>Seized by Death's great hook,
>Such shall you *all* be!
>Everyone will be dressed in this way,
>And closed cold in clay, be he king or knight,
>In all his garments gay, that were a pretty sight;
>With many a woeful man, his flesh shall waste
>>away.

Then dreadfully and quickly,
Death will gnaw these gay knights,
Both their lungs and their lights,
Their hearts will be torn asunder
These masters most of might,
They shall be brought under,
As will you all . . .

(MARTHA *and* MARY *lead* LAZARUS *to* JESUS
*who blesses him. Exeunt*)

## SCENE 19: ENTRY INTO JERUSALEM

*The* CROWD *enters.* THREE BURGHERS *and a*
LAME MAN *are part of the Crowd. A* MESSENGER
*rushes in*

MESSENGER:
Sirs, news! Such news I have to tell!
Hither comes a man from Israel,
Close at hand, the prophet called Jesus!

BURGHER I:
And is that mighty prophet near?
Of him I have heard great marvels told.
He does great wonders, it would appear,
Healing the sick, both young and old.

BURGHER II:
Yes — five thousand men with loaves but five
He fed, and each one had enough.
He turned water into wine,
He made corn grow without a plough
Where there was none.
Dead men he restored to life —
Lazarus was one.

BURGHER III:
Truly, sirs, this is what I say,

Let us make ourselves ready now
To greet him well. Come this way
And greet him with great renown.
This is his due!

(*The* CROWD *goes to meet* JESUS, *who enters on a
donkey, attended by his* DISCIPLES. *The people
strew palm leaves in his way and shout 'Hosanna!'.
The* LAME MAN *struggles forward and confronts*
JESUS, *who throws away the crutches. The* LAME
MAN *is healed. The* CROWD *react joyfully.* JESUS
*stops the noise with a wave of his hand*)

JESUS:
I mourn for thee, I sigh, I weep,
Jerusalem to look on thee;
And so will you
That ever you your king forsook,
And were untrue.
For stone on stone will none be left,
Down to the earth will all be cast,
And all for the sins thou doest.
Thou art unkind.
Against thy king thou has trespassed,
Hold this in mind.

(*The* THREE BURGHERS *push through the Crowd*)

PETER:
See where all the Burghers draw near
Coming to worship and honour you here.

BURGHER I:
Hail, Prince of Peace that ever will endure!
Hail, loving Lord, who our cares will cure!

BURGHER II:
Hail, child of bliss in Bethlehem born!
Hail, Lord that shaped both day and morn!

BURGHER III:

Hail, conqueror! Hail, most of might!
Hail, pitiful! Hail, lovely light!

ALL THREE:

Hail, our saviour!

(JESUS *turns away in sorrow.* JUDAS *kisses him*)

JUDAS:

Hail, King of the Jews!

(JESUS *weeps but the* CROWD *takes up the chant —
'Hail, Jesus! King of the Jews!' They carry him out.
JUDAS remains alone.* ANNAS, *the high priest,
enters and points after* JESUS, *holding out a bag of
money.* JUDAS *shakes his head.* ANNAS *repeats
the gesture, letting the coins jingle.* JUDAS *considers,
grabs the money and they go out*)


## SCENE 20: THE BETRAYAL

JESUS *walks in the Garden of Gethsemane with*
PETER *and* JOHN

JESUS:

Verily, I say unto thee, Peter, that this day,
Even in this night, before the cock crow twice,
Thou shalt deny me thrice.

PETER:

Nay, Master! Not I! If I should die with thee,
I would not deny thee in any wise.

JESUS:

My soul is exceeding sorrowful unto death.
Tarry ye here while I pray.

(JESUS *goes apart to pray. They doze off*)

Father, all things are possible for thee.

Take away this cup from me.
Nevertheless, not what *I* will
But what thou wilt.

(JESUS *goes back to the* DISCIPLES)

Sleepest thou? Could not thou watch one hour?
Watch ye and pray, lest ye enter into temptation.
Again I must away.

(JESUS *goes apart to pray. They doze off again*)

Father, all things are possible for thee.
Save me from the fate that awaits me.
I submit myself wholly unto thy will.

(JESUS *returns to the others*)

Rise up, let us go; lo, he that will betray me
Is at hand.

(JUDAS *enters with* SOLDIERS)

JUDAS:
Hail, Master!

JESUS:
Judas!

JUDAS:
Ah sweet Master, kiss thou me,
It is so long since I have seen thee.

(JUDAS *kisses* JESUS. *The* SOLDIERS *act on the
signal. They bind his hands and drag* JESUS *away.
Exeunt*)


## SCENE 21: THE TRIAL

CAIAPHAS *and* ANNAS *enter in good humour. The*
SOLDIERS *drag in* JESUS, *followed by a* CROWD
*baying at* JESUS

ANNAS:

>Jesus, you are most welcome to our presence.
>For him we paid Judas thirty pence.

CAIAPHAS:

>What is this doctrine that you do preach?
>Tell us here now so that others may teach.

JESUS:

>Every time I preached it was openly done,
>In the temple or synagogue where all Jews come;
>Ask them what I have said and what I have done.
>They can tell you my words.

CAIAPHAS:

>What, wretch! To whom do you speak?
>Do you talk so to the High Priest?

(FIRST JEW *strikes* JESUS)

JEW I:

>With his own mouth I have heard him say:
>Break down the temple, and on the third day
>I shall set it up again.
>Sirs, I have heard him say also
>He is the Son of God.

ANNAS:

>What say you now, Jesus?
>Speak, man, speak! Speak, idiot!
>Do you scorn to speak to me?

CAIAPHAS:

>Say whether you are God's son.

JESUS:

>God's son I am — I say not nay to thee —
>And that you shall see on the Judgement Day,
>When the Son shall come in great power and
>    majesty,
>And judge the quick and the dead.

65

CAIAPHAS:

    Out! Alas! What blasphemy is this!
    Truly, we need no more witness.
    This man is worthy to die.

CROWD:

    Yes, yes! Worthy to die!

ANNAS:

    Take him among you and beat him for sport.

(JESUS *is hurled among the* CROWD *who beat him.
They see* PETER *and thrust* JESUS *in front of him.*
PETER *shakes his head and moves away. They push*
JESUS *after him and confront* PETER *again.* PETER
*moves away. The* CROWD *pushes* JESUS *after him
and the* FIRST JEW *confronts* PETER)

JEW I:

    Sir, do you know this man?

PETER:

    Sir, I know him not — by him that made me!
    If you will believe me when I do,
    I will swear before the whole company
    That what I say is true!

(*The cock crows twice.* JESUS *looks at* PETER, *who
is shattered and leaves.* JUDAS *races in, sees* JESUS,
*hurls the money at the feet of the high priests in
disgust and races out weeping. Fanfares.* PILATE
*enters.* JESUS *is thrown in front of him*)

CAIAPHAS:

    Sir Pilate, harken to this case.
    Before you, Jesus we have brought,
    Who on our laws does bring disgrace,
    And much distress has wrought.

ANNAS:

> Yes, Sir Pilate, and worst of all,
> Defying Caesar, our Emperor renowned,
> The King of the Jews he calls himself,
> And brings our Emperor's power down.

PILATE:

> Jesus, I understand thou art a king,
> And the Son of God; thou art also
> Lord of Earth and of all things.
> Tell me if this be so.

JESUS:

> In Heaven is known my Father's intent,
> But in this world I was born.
> By my Father I was hither sent
> To comfort all who are forlorn.

PILATE:

> So, Sirs. You have heard this man. How think you?
> Consider you not, using reason,
> That what he says may well be true?
> I find in him no guilt or treason.

CAIAPHAS:

> The Emperor shall be told of this
> If you now let Jesus depart.

PILATE:

> Then tell me one thing, good sir,
> What shall be his charge?

ANNAS:

> Sir, we tell you altogether
> For his evil works we have brought him hither.

PILATE:

> Take him to your own court,
> Judge him after your law, as you ought.

CAIAPHAS:
    For us it is not lawful
    To execute a criminal;
    That is why we bring him thus —
    For he shall not be king over us!

CROWD:
    No, No! Long live Caesar!

PILATE:
    Jesus, art thou King of the Jews?

JESUS:
    So you say.

PILATE:
    Tell me then, where is your kingdom?

JESUS:
    My kingdom is not of this world.
    If it had been thus,
    I had never been delivered like this.

PILATE:
    Sirs, find some other judge if you can —
    I see no error in this man.

    (ANNAS *hands* PILATE *a scroll*)

ANNAS:
    Sir Pilate, this list of crimes now see
    And discover much mischief in this man,
    Which all these people will prove — they can!
    From here to the land of Galilee.

CROWD:
    Yes! Yes! Yes!

PILATE:
    Sirs, one thing is clear to me,
    If Jesus were born in Galilee,

The judgement of him lies not with me.
Herod is the king of that country.
Therefore take him and with speed,
To Herod the King you must him lead,
And say I commend myself in word and deed.

(*He hands back the scroll and exits. Enter* HEROD)

CAIAPHAS:

Hail, Herod, most excellent king!
We are commanded here in your presence.
Pilate sends to you his greeting,
And Jesus that has done great offence.

ANNAS:

My sovereign Lord, he corrupts the law,
And if he continues ten months more,
He will destroy your people and rule.

HEROD:

Now, by Mahomet, my god of grace!
This deed of Pilate's is very kind.
I forgive him now his trespasses,
And forever shall be his friend . . .
Jesus, welcome to this place,
I have long desired to see your face,
To have knowledge of what your miracles meant.
I have heard great wonders of thee,
You make lepers whole and fair to sight,
And they that are dead restore to life,
Now, Jesus, let me see,
A miracle wrought especially for me.

(JESUS *remains silent*)

In haste now, do it in with diligence,
For you are in my presence.

(JESUS *is silent.* HEROD *angers*)

69

Jesus, why do you not speak to your king?
What is the cause of your staying so still?
I am the judge of all things here —
Your life and death lie at my will.

CAIAPHAS:
Sire, this is but a clever ruse.
He will only speak when he choose.

HEROD:
What, you unhanged heathen! Will you say nothing?
Do you fear to speak before your king?

ANNAS:
No, he is not fearful but full of guile,
So that we may not accuse him.

HEROD:
Speak, you foul slave! Damn you with curses!
Look up! The devil will teach you!
Sirs — beat his body bare with scourges,
And make him speak.

(SOLDIERS *pull his robe off and hold him ready for the whip. Another* SOLDIER *whips him but* JESUS *remains silent. In fear,* HEROD *interrupts*)

Cease, I command you in the name of hell!
His errors never will he tell.
Sirs, take Jesus without more pain
And lead him back to Pilate again.
I give him power over Jesus, explain.
Take him out of my sight!

(*Exit* HEROD. *Fanfare. Enter* PILATE. JESUS *is thrown before him*)

CAIAPHAS:
Lord Pilate, the king has once more sent
Jesus to you, that you may give judgement.

PILATE:

In Jesus I find no fault, not one.
Nor does Herod since he sends him on.

JEW I:

Nail him to the cross, we cry with one voice!

CROWD:

Nail him! Nail him to the cross!

PILATE:

You men — for shame! Silence your noise.
My counsel will I say.
You know the custom, each one here,
That I release to you a prisoner
On the Feast that is drawing near,
In honour of the day.
Shall it be Jesus?

JEW I:

No! He is worthy to suffer death!
And so we cry with one breath —
Barabbas be reprieved!

CROWD:

Barabbas! Barabbas!

PILATE:

You priests, Caiaphas and Annas now,
What will you do? Will you let him go?

CAIAPHAS:

No — condemn him!

ANNAS:

Nail him to the cross!

PILATE:

Jesus, I pray you tell me now
If you be king. Say yes or no —
Are you King of the Jews?

JESUS:

>   Do you hope that this may be?
>   Or have men told you this of me?

PILATE:

>   By the gods, you know and see
>   That I am no Jew!
>   Men of your own nation
>   Call for your damnation,
>   And have done so all this day.
>   Are you King — as many say?

JESUS:

>   My realm is not of this world here,
>   No Jew would take me if it were.
>   But a king I am, I now confess,
>   That came down to earth to bear witness
>   Of truth, and therefore was I born.
>   And all that live in truthfulness,
>   Listen and do not scorn.

PILATE:

>   Tell me, Jesus, what is the truth?

JESUS:

>   It comes from God's own goodness.

PILATE:

>   On earth, then, truth may not exist,
>   Is that your opinion?

JESUS:

>   How can truth live on earth, tell me,
>   When thus condemned on earth is he,
>   By those who have authority
>   On earth over reason?

PILATE:

>   Lords, I find no cause I fear
>   To sentence this man that stands here.

CAIAPHAS:
> Four reasons seem quite clear to me
> For which this man deserves to die.
> One — that he wants to be our King.
> Two — on the Sabbath morning
> He ceases not the sick to free.
> Three — our temple will come falling
> But he will build it high again!
> Four — he has profaned it!

ANNAS:
> Sir Pilate, judge now wisely, use your wits.
> Condemn this Jesus before you quit,
> Upon the cross to suffer pain!
> Lord Pilate, Prince without peer,
> He should not go unpunished here,
> Let him suffer death!

CROWD:
> Crucify him! Crucify him!

CAIAPHAS:
> Now, sir, do as we say you must.
> Condemn to death this Jesus.
> Or to Caesar we shall entrust him,
> And make your friendship cold.

PILATE:
> In token that I am guiltless of this blood,
> You shall watch
> While both my hands are washed.

> (*He signals a* SERVANT, *who brings a bowl of water and a towel.* PILATE *slowly washes his hands*)

> This blood shall be dearly bought, I warn you,
> That you spill so freely.

JEW I:
> We pray that it may fall endlessly
> On us and on our company!

CROWD:
> Yes, yes! On us let it fall!

PILATE:
> Now your desires I shall fulfil,
> Take him away among you all.
> On a cross nail him well,
> And make his ending there.

(JESUS *is hurled to the* CROWD *who rush out with him. A thoughtful* PILATE *is last to leave*)

## *SCENE 22: THE CRUCIFIXION*

TWO TORTURERS *enter, carrying hammers, nails, ropes*

TORTURER I:
> All peace, all peace among you all!
> And see you now what shall befall
> This false knave here,
> That with his high and mighty boasts
> Has thought himself as wise as God,
> Among us many a year.

(JESUS *enters, dragging the cross towards Calvary.* TWO MORE TORTURERS *flank him. One kicks and one whips him*)

TORTURER II:
> He calls himself a prophet, too,
> And say he can cure all ills for you!
> Before long we shall soon know
> If he can conquer his own woe.
> See now where he comes.

74

**TORTURER III:**

> Was it not a wondrous thing
> That he dare to call himself king,
> And build so great a lie?
> By Mahomet, while I live
> Those proud words I will never forgive,
> Till he be hanged on high.

**TORTURER IV:**

> I shall work with all my might
> To crush his pride this very night.
> Though he pretends he would do no ill,
> He can, always, when he will.

*(JESUS reaches Calvary and lays down the cross, exhausted. TORTURER I harries the others.)*

**TORTURER I:**

> Come on, make haste! Let us teach this thief
> What means we have of bringing death.
> Indeed, sir, since you call yourself king,
> You must prove worthy of that rank
> And ride into war.
> You must joust in tournament,
> So sit you fast, for we are bent
> On tying you to your horse.

**TORTURER III:**

> If you be king, we will earn a medal
> For none shall knock you from your saddle.
> Prepare to mount — be bold!

*(They lift JESUS and lay him on the cross)*

**TORTURER IV:**

> Stand close now, friends, and let us see
> How we can horse this king so free
> Upon this nag so cold.
> You stand there over on that side,

And we shall see how he can ride,
And how he bears a shaft.

(*He flicks* TORTURER III *with his rope to hurry him into position.* TORTURER III *grabs him.* TORTURER I *stops the fight*)

TORTURER I:
Sirs, come hither and have done!

(TORTURERS III *and* IV *stand at either end of the cross piece to tie* JESUS's *arms to the wood*)

TORTURER II:
You tie a knot with all your strength
And draw his arm out to full length
Till it comes to the bore.

(TORTURER III *ties one of* JESUS's *wrists to the wood*)

TORTURER IV:
Bind up tight that band,
I will help with this other hand
And see what I can do.

(TORTURER IV *does the same as* III *but finds the latter has pulled* JESUS's *arm too far in one direction*)

You are stupid, man!

TORTURER III:
Who is stupid?

TORTURER IV:
Thee.
It needs, as any craftsman can see,
Half his span, not more

TORTURER I:
Hold down his knees.

76

TORTURER II:
   I'll do that with ease.

TORTURER I:
   Draw down his legs and fix those bands.

(TORTURER II *draws down the legs and lashes them to the cross.* TORTURERS III *and* IV *now have a tug-of-war with* JESUS's *arms*)

   No, fellows! It is no game.
   Both of you must pull the same!
   Bind his arms, I say.

(*They do so properly this time.* TORTURER I *gets out hammers and nails*)

   Hold him steady — see his hands lie flat.
   Now through them will I drive a nail.
   I promise that it will not fail
   To tear the palm apart.

TORTURER IV:
   That will I do! Let me start!

TORTURER III:
   Let me do it!

TORTURER IV:
   If you can!

TORTURER III:
   I am the better man!

TORTURER I:
   Hold your noise and both begin.

(TORTURERS III *and* IV *take the hammers and nail a hand each to the cross. No sound from* JESUS)

TORTURER I:
   Hold his knees, now his feet . . . here, you,
   Take the hammer and nail them through.

(TORTURER II *hammers a nail through* JESUS's *feet as his colleagues hold the legs down*)

TORTURER III:
　　So — that is well.

TORTURER IV:
　　It will stand the test.

TORTURER I:
　　Now let me see who will give his best
　　Of all his might and force.

　　(*They start to lift the cross up*)

TORTURER IV:
　　Lift, lift!

TORTURER III:
　　Go on!

TORTURER II:
　　Again! Now more!

TORTURER I:
　　Up with the timber!

TORTURER II:
　　Now let it rest.

TORTURER I:
　　Keep it steady, one and all.

TORTURER IV:
　　Into the hole now let it fall,
　　And then it is sure to stand.

　　(*The cross sinks into the hole. They secure it with wedges and stand back to admire their handiwork*)

TORTURER I:
　　Right up, my friends. It is well done.

TORTURER IV:
>You up there — stare at the sun!

TORTURER III:
>Now, great king, where is your crown?

TORTURER II:
>Do you think you will ever come down?

TORTURER I:
>Make sure it is fast.

(TORTURER II *checks the wedges*)

TORTURER II:
>Now it stands up like a mast!
>I wager he and his steed so high
>Will not part tonight.

(TORTURER I *leads them out.* JESUS *is alone*)

JESUS:
>I pray you people that pass by
>And lead your lives so pleasantly,
>Heave up your hearts on high.
>Who now did ever see a body
>So buffeted and beaten bloody,
>And racked by such despair?
>My power, my glory and my might
>Are nought but sorrow to the sight.
>No comfort now but care.
>My people, what have I done to ye
>That thus you have all tortured me?
>How have I wronged you, answer me,
>That you have nailed me to a tree
>For errors that are yours?
>But Father high upon thy throne,
>Forgive them all their guilt.
>They do not know what they have done,
>Nor why my blood is spilt.

(JESUS *hangs his head down. Enter* MARY *and* JOHN)

MARY:

Why do you hang so high, my son?
Great sorrow through me spreads.
With tears of pain your face does run,
I see your body bleed.
Oh, son, why must you leave me so?
On earth there can be no
Comfort for all this ill.

JOHN:

Gentle Mary, it is his will
That he should suffer cruel pain
And die upon a tree,
And to life shall rise again.
On the third day it should be.

MARY:

Ah Death, what have you done?
I had no child save one,
Best under sun and moon,
Good Lord, grant me this boon,
And let me not live on.
Gone is all my joy and bliss,
My death must follow his —
My sweet son, have mercy!

(MARY *weeps and embraces the foot of the cross*)

JESUS:

My mother mild, now stop your crying,
Since mankind throughout my dying
May thus to bliss be brought.
The pain I suffer is savage here,
But this grief of mine, my mother dear,
Martyrs me much more.

Take there, John, as your child.
John, see here your mother mild.

(JOHN *helps* MARY *up and leads her out. The*
FOUR TORTURERS *enter. They have been drinking.*
*One of them carries a sponge and a spear*)

TORTURER I:
Are you thirsty now? Here is a drink.
It is not very sweet, I think.

(TORTURER I *puts the sponge on the spear and lifts*
*it up to* JESUS*'s face.* JESUS *takes the drink, only to*
*find it is vinegar. He turns away. The men laugh*)

TORTURER II:
Now, sir, speak what you will.

TORTURER III:
Yet if you had kept quiet and still,

TORTURER IV:
You would not be in this state.

TORTURER III:
He said he was King of the Jews.

TORTURER IV:
But by this time that claim he rues.

TORTURER II:
He shut his mouth too late.
So for his lies, to serve him right,
Share out his clothes, every mite,
Come now, let us start.

TORTURER III:
As ever well I hope to fare,
Straight will we his mantle tear,
And each man take a part.

TORTURER I:
> Why not go on my advice?
> Sit we round and throw a dice —
> That gives a chance to all.

(*They form a circle below the cross. They speak as they throw the dice in turn*)

TORTURER II:
> Here's mine.

TORTURER III:
> Now mine.

TORTURER IV:
> A double one!

TORTURER I:
> Now, Mahomet, on thee I call!

TORTURER IV:
> Ya! Now me! (*he throws*) 'Tis mine! Have done!

(*He grabs the robe from the floor*)

TORTURER I:
> Well, since it looks as if you won,
> I will bargain for it — right?

(TORTURERS I *and* IV *haggle in the background. The others look up at* JESUS)

TORTURER III:
> If you are the man that men call Christ,
> Come down among us from your height —
> Do not suffer in that way.

TORTURER II:
> He raised Lazarus from the grave
> But himself he cannot save,
> Now in his greatest need.

82

JESUS:

My God, my God — why hast thou forsaken me!

TORTURER I:

I think he will soon be dead,
His heart is burst — behold!

JESUS:

Now is my passion at an end.
Father in Heaven, into your hands
I here commit my soul.

(JESUS *dies*. TORTURER I *throws the spear to* III,
*who sinks it into* JESUS*'s side. At that moment,*
*thunder rolls. Blackout.*)


## SCENE 23: THE RESURRECTION

PILATE, ANNAS *and* CAIAPHAS *hurry in, alarmed.*
*While they speak,* JESUS *is taken down from the*
*cross at Calvary*

PILATE:

Most mighty of estate,
As my name is Sir Pilate,
Honoured by rule and by degree,
I gave leave to hang
Jesus on a tree.
Yet fear I lest he will us grieve.
For what I saw I may well believe.
I saw the stones begin to cleave
And dead men to heave.
And therefore, Sir Caiaphas, I dread
Lest there be peril in this deed.
I saw him hang on the rood and bleed
Till all his blood was shed.
But just when he would his death take,
The sky became wondrous black.

Lightning, thunder, the earth began to quake.
I fear more dread will come.

ANNAS:
I saw him and his company
Raise men with sorcery,
Who long before were dead.
Lest his body be ta'en away,
Guard it with all good speed.

CAIAPHAS:
That no shame to us fall,
Let us ordain among us all,
To guard the corpse.

PILATE:
Sirs, with this counsel I agree,
Orders have I given already
To watch him lowered from his tree
And put into his tomb.
Now I have sworn my knights will die,
If Christ from his grave do fly.

(*Enter the* CENTURION, *nervous and shaking*)

CENTURION.
Harken, Sir Pilate.
Jesus that was on Friday slain,
Through his might is risen again
This third day.
There came no power to take him away.
But such a sleep on us he set,
We could do nought, my lord, but let
Him rise and go his way.

PILATE:
Now by my oath to Caesar sworn!
If you and others secretly
Sold him to his company,
You all deserve to die!

84

CENTURION:
> He rose up, as I said just now,
> And left us lying — I know not how,
> But we were all amazed.

PILATE:
> Fie upon thee! Thy trust is full bare!
> Fly hence fast! I counsel you fair!

CENTURION:
> That time when he his way took,
> I neither dared to speak nor look,
> But lay in the soundest dream.

PILATE:
> Fie on thee, thou tainted dog!
> What! Lay you still in that place
> And let that flatterer go, you rogue!

CAIAPHAS:
> Do not trust what you have heard.
> How honest is that soldier's word?
> And were it true, be not afeard.
> He cannot hurt us now.

ANNAS:
> Sir Bishop, I tell you truly,
> This foolish prophet that we sent to die,
> Through his own witchcraft is stolen away.

PILATE:
> Now, in good faith, full woe is me
> That he has risen thus privily.

(A CROWD *enters as music swells.* JESUS *appears above.* PILATE, CAIAPHAS *and* ANNAS *leave, but the* CROWD *falls to its knees*)

JESUS:
> Men of earth, whom I have wrought,

Now awake and slumber not!
Thou hast with bitter grief been bought,
And been made free.
I made thee clean, O sinful man.
With pain and sorrow wast thou won.
From heart and side the blood did run,
So racked and torn.
Thou shouldst love me who gave you then
My life for yours.
See how I hold my arms out wide
Ready to save thee, ever to abide;
My love never has denied thee,
That thou must have known.
But now I desire that some return
Of love to me be shown;
I ask thy love, but that one thing,
And that you strive to flee from sin,
And live in charity with men.
Then in my bliss
Thou shalt remain
Always.

*One by one the people start to cry 'Te Deum
Laudamus' and the place fills with holy light.
Then all exit in silence.* JESUS *is left alone, arms still
stretched out wide.*
*Blackout.*

## THE END